Tim Mallett

On How to Be

UTTERLY BRILLIANT

Illustrated by Ashley Haynes

Piccolo Books
A Piccolo Original

THIS BOOK IS DEDICATED TO ...

... with utterly special thanks to Aisling O'Hagan

First published 1989 by Pan Books Ltd,
Cavaye Place, London SW10 9PG

9 8 7 6 5 4 3 2 1

© Timmy Mallett, 1989
Designed by Jo Speakman

ISBN 0 330 30909 9

Printed in Great Britain by Richard Clay Ltd, Bungay, Suffolk

CONGRATULATIONS !

you have just achieved your first utterly brilliant achievement! You have opened this utterly brilliant book!! (wow! yeah! fanfares, tarantaras etc... other sound effects supplied in shop!) and you are now a mere 96 utterly brilliant pages and 16 utterly sticky stickers away from closing it and joining the ranks of the world's most utterly brilliant people (me and Magic)! Can you wait? Neither can I – so get going......

 immy ! (Magic)   Squawk!

ON YOUR MARKS
GET SET
TURN THE PAGE
GO

THIS BOOK BELONGS TO:

....

NAME ....

ADDRESS ....

ATROUSERS ....

PLANET ....

SIZE OF HEAD ....

NUMBER OF SPOTS ....

FAVOURITE ARM PIT ....

FAVOURITE MISSING TOOTH ....

LONGEST TOE NAIL ....

LONGEST NOSTRIL ....

BEST KNEE ....

BEST HEIGHT ....
(on tiptoes with arms stretched up)

BEST STAIN ON SCHOOL UNIFORM ....

BEST HANKIE ....

BEST NUMBER ....

BEST FRIEND ....

4

BEST TIME OF DAY ....

BEST TELLY PROGRAMME ....

BEST PERSON YOU'D MOST LIKE TO SHAKE,
RATTLE AND ROLL WITH ....

BEST EVER FRY-UP ....

BEST EXCUSE ....

BEST STRAIGHT LINE ....

BEST LIGHT SWITCH ....

BEST AGE YOU'D MOST LIKE TO BE ....

BEST AND MOST IMPORTANT THING IN THE
WORLD ....

BEST SHORT CUT ....

BEST SECRET ....

BEST SMELL ....

BEST BEST ....

BEST BEST BEST ....

BEST WORST ....

BEST JOKE
....
....

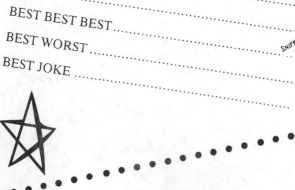

HOW TO LOOK

✗ *UTTERLY BRILLIANT*

First of all make sure you always wear something that other people will recognize you by. Most of the important people in the world have taken my advice on this one. The Queen, for instance is instantly recognized by her crown, Boris Becker, by his tennis racquet, Michael Jackson, for always wearing someone else's face and me, by the utterly brilliant glasses wrapped round my head. '

Secondly, throw out your old wardrobe (if it won't fit through your bedroom window, make a hole in the floor and slide it down into the living room. If this fails, eat it).

WHAT'S WHITE AND WEARS CHECKED TROUSERS? RUPERT THE FRIDGE!!–

In order to BE utterly brilliant you've got to LOOK utterly brilliant Here are some suggestions...

VITALLY IMPORTANT THINGS FOR YOUR

UTTERLY BRILLIANT NEW WARDROBE

HANGING SPACE. Make sure your wardrobe has enough room for you to hang around in. A sofa and a TV are handy for those mornings when you need time to choose your outfit.

BOOKS. For the days when you need to look brainy. But remember, you can't judge a book by its cover, so if it looks boring – rip it off. You'll find that dictionaries make unusual little ear-rings for girls, and encyclopedias, hard-wearing shoulder pads for boys.

A FRIDGE. People are always asking me how I manage to look so cool – well, now you know.

A FLY'S COSTUME. Think of all the times you've wished you could be somewhere you're not supposed to be. Well, now you can be a fly on the wall anytime you feel like it.

A WASTE DISPOSAL UNIT. Never buy a wardrobe without one, because the next time someone you dislike asks you out – you can just say "I haven't got a thing to wear", and at the press of a button, you won't have. A WAIST Disposal also comes in handy if you've got any fat friends.

A BIRTHDAY SUIT. Brilliant for wearing in the bath, and for all those occasions where you really want to be noticed.

WHAT TO EAT TO BE

UTTERLY BRILLIANT

In order to be utterly brilliant you need to eat, and the best thing to eat is food.

(For this you need a mouth, teeth, a tongue and food). Lift food up, open mouth, shove food in, chew and swallow.

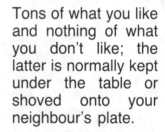

Tons of what you like and nothing of what you don't like; the latter is normally kept under the table or shoved onto your neighbour's plate.

Constantly, only stopping to swallow.

Anywhere where there's food.

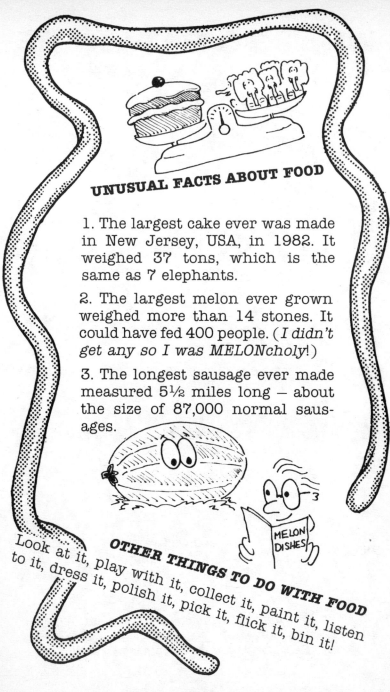

UNUSUAL FACTS ABOUT FOOD

1. The largest cake ever was made in New Jersey, USA, in 1982. It weighed 37 tons, which is the same as 7 elephants.

2. The largest melon ever grown weighed more than 14 stones. It could have fed 400 people. (*I didn't get any so I was MELONcholy!*)

3. The longest sausage ever made measured 5½ miles long — about the size of 87,000 normal sausages.

OTHER THINGS TO DO WITH FOOD

Look at it, play with it, collect it, paint it, listen to it, dress it, polish it, pick it, flick it, bin it!

9

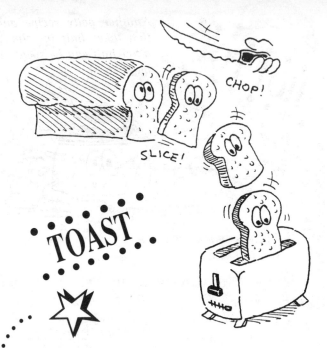

Toast is one of my favourite meals and one that I can normally rustle up in under an hour.

● Go to a shop that sells BREAD and buy some that has been cut into SLICES.

● Take 2 slices (or more if you have other guests) and place them in the toaster. If you do not have a toaster, hard luck.

● Switch it on and wait 25 minutes till nice and crisp. You can sing or hum quietly to yourself while waiting but I normally find this disturbs concentration.

● When toast pops up, pick it up from floor and serve with a spread of your own choice. Bedspreads are very popular with my friends.

HOT POT

Another potty recipe and one that takes half the time. (The other half can be spent making more toast.)

● Buy a sauna (one that is suitable for Hot Pots).

● Turn it on to full temperature and allow it to heat up.

● Place pot in centre of sauna for 2 days.

● Remove and serve with cold water.

KITTY FRITTERS

This is Magic's favourite recipe.

11

APPLE TURNOVER

● Go and buy an apple. If this is difficult you can grow your own, but it may take a little longer. Check it's an apple first by eating it – then go and buy another, checking it again.

● Take the apple to your nearest swimming pool and place it on the farthest end of the diving board.

● Put your swimming trunks on. Climb up onto the diving board (the one with the apple on it). Stand behind the apple and jump up and down very quickly, being careful not to fall in.

● The apple should fall off the board, turn over in mid-flight and land at the bottom of the swimming pool. If this does not happen, try another swimming pool.

JUST A COUPLE OF EXTRA STRANGE FACTS ABOUT EATING

1. The duck-billed platypus eats its own weight in worms every day. (I wonder if the worm eats its own weight in duck-billed platypus!)

2. The world record for eating daffodils is held by a Yorkshire woman who, in 1972, gobbled down 60 heads in 26.5 seconds, (she only comes out in Spring!).

UTTERLY BRILLIANT

The first thing I do when I get up in the morning is decide where I'm going to go to be utterly brilliant. After all, you're never going to get anywhere staying indoors (unless you live in a mobile home). You've got to see – and be seen in all the right places at all the right times. So get going.

THINGS I KNOW THAT YOU DON'T ABOUT THE WORLD

✗ The world's population is about 6,000 million – but is increasing by 216,000 daily, this means that by the time you have finished reading this chapter – 450 babies will have been born. (What a nappy thought!)

✗ There are more men than women in the world. (I should know – I counted.)

✗ Before the year 582, people thought that the world was flat. (Someone sailed off the edge to make double sure.)

IT'S THE EDGE OF THE WORLD!

NO IT'S NOT... IT'S THE BOTTOM OF THE PAGE!

HELP!

✘ The first ever atlas of the world was drawn in the year 1585. (And coloured in by Charles I on a rainy afternoon.)

✘ The remotest place on earth is a volcanic island in the South Atlantic called Tristan de Cunha. (My great Uncle plays bingo there every Friday night.)

✘ The Vatican City in Rome is the smallest country in the world and has a population of only 1,000 people. (And a Pope.)

✘ The largest populated country is China – which has over 1032 million inhabitants. (And a lot of rice.)

All utterly brilliant people have a hobby, and the most common hobby in the entire universe is collecting things. So the next step to becoming utterly brilliant is to collect something.

THINGS TO COLLECT TO BE UTTERLY BRILLIANT

HELPFUL HINT

The first thing to do here is to make sure that what you collect is not boring. Collecting boring things is boring and will not be any fun.
Stamps and coins are the obvious boring choice, but firstly, no one has ever become famous for this and secondly, it's boring!. Look out for other boring collections like:—

USED WRAPPING PAPER. An unbelievably huge number of mums collect this, and have you ever been given a pressie wrapped in used paper? No. My suggestion is to change your mum and throw the wrapping paper in the bin.

CARDBOARD TUBES. Even more boring, unless you can collect enough to make your own Channel Tunnel.

RUBBER BANDS. The best thing to do with rubber bands, if you really want to collect them, is to put them all together in a box, and then put the box somewhere you can't find it.

MARBLES. Most people end up losing them!

Sounds pretty normal but have you ever thought how difficult it is to lose a pair of socks. You only ever lose one of them. So a good way of getting famous is to hold an annual international odd sock reunion where lonely socks can meet up with their partner without feeling a HEEL. It would certainly give you a FOOT in the door anyway.

THE ODD SOCK
→ BALL ←
GRAND SOCK REUNION

SOCK-AROUND THE CLOCK

DREAM Nº 177

OTHER UNUSUAL COLLECTIONS

A woman in America has been collecting dreams for over 16 years and has a total of 2,500 including her own.

(Must be a nightmare.)

The world's largest collection of vacuum cleaners is owned by a Swiss man who, after three years, has a total of 80.

(He's a sucker for dust.)

A Lancashire man owns the world's largest collection of bricks — a selection of more than 3,420.

(I've got more than that in my house.)

An American man started collectiong old oil rags back in the 1950's and now owns a vast collection of over 13,000.

(Is that oil?)

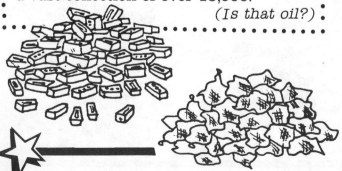

The way to become famous through your collection is to make sure you collect something that's a bit strange and, on the whole pretty useless. For example:-

BEDS

LOUIS SNORES HERE

BED Nº 144

Again this sounds quite normal but have you ever known anyone to have more than one bed? – apart from King Louis XIV who had the largest ever collection of 413 – all dotted about his kingdom so that wherever he travelled he could sleep in his own bed.

My own collection of beds includes a flower bed (for the flowers), a water bed (for my water) and a bed of nails (for my mallet).

This is a really interesting thing to collect because it's always growing. 'Things to do' never ceases to be an endless challenge. Normally the 'Things to do' collection lives in your room under the bed, or on top of a cupboard where you can't see it. But the great thing is that if you get bored with it you can swop it with a friend, and that way it will never get done and everyone will be happy.

THINGS TO DO

BY THE WAY
My favourite hobby is collecting hobbies. So far I have 827½. Some of them are really valuable! If you have any spare hobbies – do you want to swap?

HOW TO MAKE THE MOST UTTERLY BRILLIANT FRIENDS IN THE LEAST TIME

* Tell everyone you live in a sweet shop.
* Advertise in the local paper (offer a reward).
* Make your own friends out of wax and cotton wool.
* Circulate a computer test to everyone in the world. It should contain the following questions:-

WHAT WOULD YOU DO WITH A FRIEND IF YOU HAD ONE?

a) Have him dry cleaned and pressed, ready to wear at a minute's notice.

b) Go on a world cruise, without him.

c) Bounce him up and down in a cow pat.

d) Take him for long walks in a cupboard.

ARE YOU THE SORT OF FRIEND THAT

a) Goes parachute jumping with a piano in your rucksack.

b) Puts toothpaste on your cornflakes to save time in the morning.

c) Would feel uncomfortable walking into a department store without any clothes on.

d) Would take a fish for swimming lessons.

WHAT DO YOU LOOK FOR IN A FRIEND ?

a) Pimples.

b) Someone to do your homework for you.

c) Someone who will take the blame for absolutely anything.

d) Someone with an identical face so that you can be in more than two places at one time.

HOW WOULD YOU DESCRIBE YOURSELF ?

a) Pretty smartish.

b) Competent and capable.

c) Incompetent but capable.

d) Incapable but uncompetent

WHAT UTTERLY BRILLIANT PETS TO KEEP

An utterly brilliant person needs an utterly brilliant companion, and what could be better than a pet? A pet is a fantastic companion and far more useful than a friend. I mean for a start you can't buy a friend in a pet shop, you can't take a friend out on a lead, you can't put a friend in a glass bowl or a pond, and you can't teach a friend to fly, like Magic.

So – here are some utterly brilliant ideas for an utterly brilliant companion –

PET ROCK

This can be found either in your garden or at the seaside. They come in all sizes and colours, they don't eat much and will never run off with the cat next door. The best thing about a pet rock is that it will stay wherever you put it and go wherever you want it to go. Make sure you don't get one that's too big though, or it won't fit through the cat flap.

PET SHOE

A shoe can make a brilliant pet, as my great uncle the Duke of Wellington used to tell me. You and your shoe can become real SOLE mates. All the shoes I've had have never left my feet and have always TOED the line. Again it's important to get the right sized pet shoe, and not one that's going to look daft on a lead, like a ballet shoe or a flip flop. Try taking one out for a walk and telling it to 'heel'.

WHO WEARS THE LARGEST SHOES IN THE WORLD?
THE PERSON WITH THE LARGEST FEET!

WHAT DID KYLIE MINOGUE SAY TO HER PET DUCK?
I SHOULD BE SO CLUCKY!

One of my ancestors, King Arthur, had a pet table and he's never looked back. The ones with 4 legs are the best, and if you're looking for the kind of pet that won't get in your parents way, why not get one that you can fold up and put away in the cupboard. And another thing, pet tables love to play board games.

PET TABLE

PET EAR

This is a rather difficult pet to keep, as a friend normally comes with it. However it can be jolly good fun. It was my great great grandfather Julius Caesar who gave me this idea, when he said to his subjects 'Friends, Romans, country-men, lend me your ears,' and they did. Ears are great for listening to your boastings, eavesdrop-ping on other people's conversations and answering the telephone for you when you are out.

PET WHALE

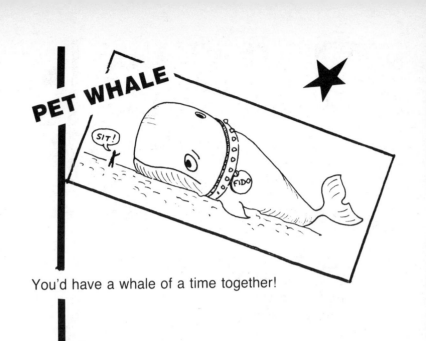

You'd have a whale of a time together!

HISTORICAL FACTS ABOUT PETS

1. Helen of Troy had a pet wooden horse who came in very handy.

2. Hannibal used his pet elephant to help him conquer Rome (he took his trunk with him.)

3. Hercules was very fond of lions, (and he was always lion around!)

4. Cleopatra never went anywhere without her asps.

STRANGE FACTS ABOUT ANIMALS

1. The cat is the only animal — other than the camel and giraffe — to walk by moving its front and hind legs on one side, then on the other. (*All the others go by car.*)

2. The electric eel of South America is the most powerful electric fish — producing 550 volts in its tail which it uses to stun or kill nearby fish. (*What I want to know is can it change a plug?*)

3. The saying 'An elephant never forgets' is more true than you'd think. Elephants are extremely intelligent and, properly trained, can understand up to 30 commands. (*Yeah — well Magic can do 31.*)

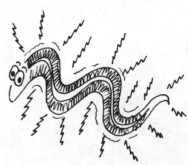

4. A horse can look back with one eye while looking forwards with the other. *(No wonder they never know if they're coming or going.)*

5. Cows have unique stomachs with four sections. Once they have swallowed food they bring it up into their mouths again for a second chew. The food is then swallowed again and passed into their second stomach to be digested. *(Yuck!!! fancy another chew at last week's school dinner?)*

6. When alarmed, a squid squirts a cloud of black ink into the water. This acts as a smokescreen behind which the squid can escape. *(How much does it cost?)*

Now that I've given you some ideas about utterly brilliant pets I'm going to let you in on a few secrets about my utterly brilliant pet-Magic.

A DAY IN THE LIFE OF

UTTERLY BRILLIANT

MAGIC

★★★

What a lot of you don't know is that Magic is not the quiet, well behaved, dumb bird he appears to be on tv, but is in fact a noisy, athletic, greedy and highly intelligent cockatiel. But he knows who's master at Timmy Towers. Here is a typical day in the life of Magic.

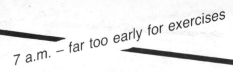

35

UTTERLY INTERESTING FACTS ABOUT ME

BORN: At a very early age. In fact I was just a baby.

PLACE OF BIRTH: A bed, in the bedroom, not far from the window where I had an utterly brilliant view of the curtains.

DATE OF BIRTH My birthday, October 18th (send presents and make them big).

PARENTS: Mr and Mrs Mallett (stupid!)

SCHOOL: Never heard of it!

BUSINESS: None of yours.

HOBBIES: Being famous, going 'bleugh', arguing with myself about who's better — me or me, flicking peas, splitting hairs, painting and slurping drinks.

INTERESTS: Me, caravan spotting, being messy, stink collecting, walking with a seat belt on, watching traffic lights change, toenail sculpture and hot water bottle bouncing.

FAVOURITE PERSON: Me

FAVOURITE BOOK: This one.

FAVOURITE FILM: Any one with me in it.

FAVOURITE PAINTING: A self-portrait I did of myself.

FAVOURITE SONG: 'Me myself I'

FAVOURITE FOOD: Anything as long as there's lots of it, except meat or leeks.

FAVOURITE CHARACTER IN HISTORY: Me.

That's enough about me. Here is some space for you to write about yourself: →

THE UTTERLY BRILLIANT
WORLD OF TV

Probably the most utterly brilliant,
earth liquidizing, planet prodding, universe crumbling thing you can ever
do, is to get yourself on TV – like me.
But before you do that, you will need
to know a few utterly brilliant facts
about it.

FACTS ABOUT TV

● Television was invented by a man named John Logie Baird in 1925. *(hence the cartoon Yogi Bear.*

● The first person to appear on TV was a 15-year-old boy named Bill Taynton.
(It should have been me but I was busy.)

● There are now more than 250 million TV sets in the world.

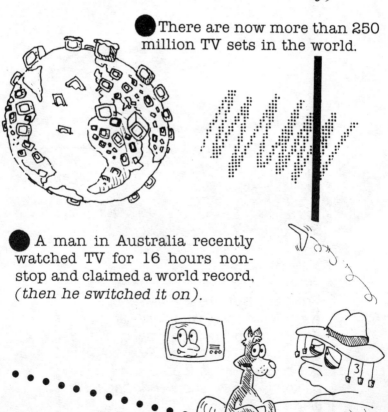

● A man in Australia recently watched TV for 16 hours non-stop and claimed a world record, *(then he switched it on).*

42

● Colour TV was first transmitted in 1929, by an American man named Herbert Ives.
(*Herbert Ives had 7 wives, his 7 wives had 777,0000 handbags.*)

● My utterly brilliant face has spent approximately 156,000 utterly brilliant minutes squashed inside a TV screen.
(*Gosh I'm utterly beautiful!*)

● The person who has appeared most on TV is the test-card girl (*but she still hasn't been on Wacaday*).

● Make sure you've got one. If you haven't, get a pair of binoculars or ask your dad if you can move next door to a TV shop.

● Make it feel important by putting it in a prominent place in the living room, arranging all the furniture around it and staring at it all day (except when you're asleep).

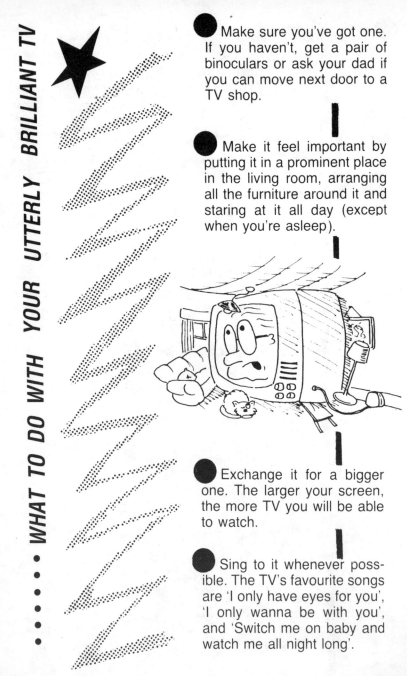

● Exchange it for a bigger one. The larger your screen, the more TV you will be able to watch.

● Sing to it whenever possible. The TV's favourite songs are 'I only have eyes for you', 'I only wanna be with you', and 'Switch me on baby and watch me all night long'.

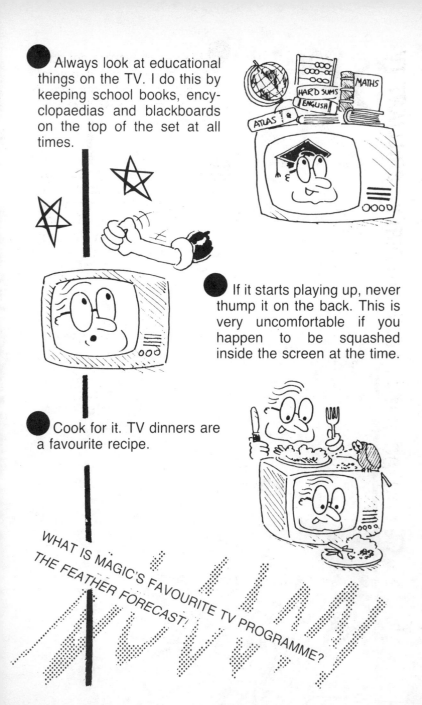

Always look at educational things on the TV. I do this by keeping school books, encyclopaedias and blackboards on the top of the set at all times.

If it starts playing up, never thump it on the back. This is very uncomfortable if you happen to be squashed inside the screen at the time.

Cook for it. TV dinners are a favourite recipe.

WHAT IS MAGIC'S FAVOURITE TV PROGRAMME? THE FEATHER FORECAST!

45

ARE YOU UTTERLY BRILLIANT YET?

Not until you've passed the Mallet Master-mind Examination. You've got exactly 20 seconds to answer these utterly brilliant questions. And no cheating!

HISTORY

1. Who was the real king of England?

   a) Ethelred the Unready
   b) Wilfred the Everready
   c) Alfred the Neverready
   d) Mildred the 'I'll be there in a minute'.

2. What did William Tell shoot from his son's head to save Switzerland?

   a) A car
   b) A raisin
   c) An apple tree
   d) A mountain

GEOGRAPHY

1. Where does tea come from?

   a) A tea-bag
   b) A tea cloth
   c) Mr T
   d) A tea shirt

2. Where is the deepest part of the ocean?

   a) At the front
   b) At the back
   c) In the middle
   d) Round the side?

SCIENCE

1. What do you do with micro-chips?

   a) Fry them
   b) Cook them in the oven
   c) Eat them in a butty
   d) Wrap them in a newspaper and drop them in the bin

2. How does a photocopier work?

   a) Put the paper on the glass
   b) Press the button that says 'on'
   c) Wait till paper is copied
   d) Take the paper out

3. How does electricity reach the home?

   a) On foot
   b) By skateboard
   c) On the bus
   d) By taxi

SPACE

1. How hot is the sun?

   a) Not very hot
   b) Quite hot
   c) Really hot
   d) Cold

2. What is the difference between a star and a planet?

   a) A star gives autographs and a planet doesn't
   b) You can land a spaceship on a planet but not a star
   c) Planets don't act in films and stars do
   d) They are spelt differently

NATURE

1. How do cats see in the dark?

   a) Not very well
   b) They wear glasses
   c) They take a torch
   d) They turn the lights on

3. How do plants feel?

   a) OK
   b) Fine
   c) Not too good today
   d) Awful

2. What would you find on the sea bed?

   a) A continental quilt
   b) Fish-cake crumbs
   c) A hot water bottle
   d) Legs

ENGLISH

1. Complete the proverb –
   Absence makes the heart grow. . . ?

   a) Up
   b) Its nails
   c) Its own vegetables
   d) Mouldy

2. How would you ask for a
   piece of cake politely?

   a) Please could I have a
   piece of cake?
   b) May I please have a piece
   of cake?
   c) I would be delighted with
   a piece of cake
   d) Give me all of that cake
   now! Or else!

HOW TO SCORE **Use your common sense!**

HOW DID YOU SCORE? • • • • • •

0 – You obviously haven't learned a thing from this book and have absolutely no chance of ever becoming anything but completely and utterly useless. Go and lie in a bath of custard for a week. And then drink it.

1 – Pretty pathetic and fairly poor. Try reading the book instead of just colouring in the pictures.

2 – A goodish try but could do better in another twenty years.

120 – What an utterly disgusting nit of a swot you are! If you were in my class at school, I'd change schools.

ANYTHING IN BETWEEN – You've been doing the wrong quiz!

The History of Being Utterly Brilliant

Some people think that history is all about dates and stuff. But that's non-sense. (Most people only eat dates at Christmas.) History is brilliant because it's full of my utterly brave and courageous ancestors.

THE MAIN THINGS TO LOOK OUT FOR IN THE HOLY LAND ARE THE HOLES

THE HOLY LAND

Richard the Mallettheart led the famous third crusade in 1189 defending the mighty Roman empire from greedy eastern rulers, pencils and rubbers.

Robert the Bruce Springsteen of Mallett used his loyal weapon at the battle of Bannockburn in 1314, flattening a smart alec spider to save Scotland from English rule.

Henry VIII and his Six Mallets arrived about 200 years later but he got into a bit of a sticky situation trying to decide which one he wanted. The peasants were revolting and so, as my ancestors have told me, was he.

While Henry was busy being revolting in England, a couple of my other ancestors were doing pretty brilliant things in Europe.

William Shakesmallett wrote the most famous plays of all time. Mamlett, Macmallett, The Mallet of Venice, A Midsummer Night's Mallett, Much Ado about Mallett and King Henry the Mallett Part Timmy.

Napolean Bonamallett was one of the most utterly brilliant soldiers ever. He once ruled the whole of Europe but always kept his mallett hand inside his jacket, where he knew it would be safe.

Sir Francis Mallett is where I get my talent for windsurfing from. He lived in the time of Queen Elizabeth the first of two, and good old Mary Queen of Spots, and was one of the utterly greatest sea captains of all time. It was he who sank the Armada with his Armallet.

Malletangelo and his friend Mallett da Vinci were the two most utterly brilliant figures of the Renaissance. Mallettangelo spent most of his life painting ceilings (he used non-drip paint and a roller) and Da Vinci painted millions of postcards of the moaning Lisa.

Timmy the Kid the man with no mallett, had a left ear, a right ear and a wild frontier. He came riding into the twentieth century to bring law and order to the desert, and soon became the fastest mallet in the west.

WHAT'S WRAPPED IN GREASEPROOF PAPER AND SINGS 'THE BELLS, THE BELLS'?

THE LUNCH PACK OF NOTRE DAME!

WHO INVENTED FRACTIONS?

HENRY THE $\frac{1}{8}$th

GETTING INTO A HISTORY BOOK

One of the best ways of becoming utterly brilliant is to get into a history book. Here are some examples of how to do it:–

Choose a book that is big enough to get into. Cut a hole through the middle, cover yourself with grease and slide in, being careful to close the cover on the way down. Be choosy about the worms you make friends with or they will eat your words.

Become King or Queen of England. This is a bit more tricky and you need to ask your parents first. It was offered to me once but my mum said no.

Sneak into your school at night, round up all the history books, cross out every famous name and replace it with yours. No one will ever suspect.

Make your own history book by sticking lots of your own photographs into a scrapbook and making up the words. You can also use old newspapers and magazines, cutting out famous faces and using yours instead. This is an extremely boring thing to do however, and anyone caught in the act should be struck off the UTTERLY BRILLIANT list immediately!

Timmy Mallett Answers All Your Questions On How To Be Utterly Brilliant . . .

Dear Timmy,
I swim 40 lengths of the swimming pool every morning. Am I Utterly Brilliant?
Princess Diana

T. That really depends on the length of your swimming pool.

Dear Timmy
I can make my bed in under 7 seconds. Am I Utterly Brilliant?
Rick Astley

T. Could do better.

dear Timmy
I can pat my head and rub my stomach at the same time. Am I Utterly Brilliant? Sylvester Stallone!

T. Rubbish. I could do that the day I was born.

I'm a presenter on Wide Awake, a singer, a dancer and an actress. Am I Utterly Brilliant?
Michaela Strachan x

T. Absolutely not. But you do remind me of someone.

TIMMY'S MUG

INK

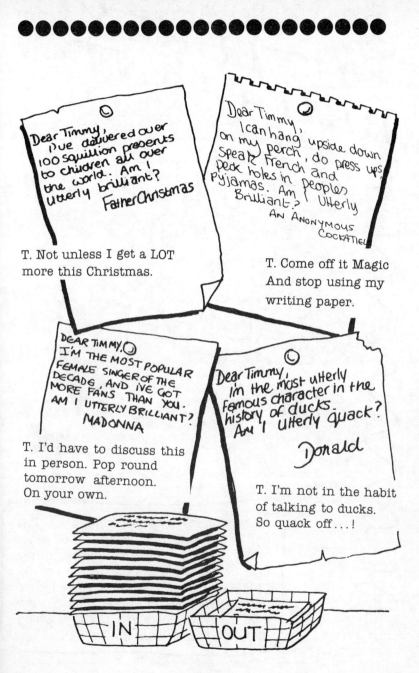

UTTERLY BRILLIANT

THINGS TO SAY

In my utterly brilliant experience I've found that you can always spot other utterly brilliant people by the way they talk. Sentences like 'Look at me I'm the greatest, most outstandingly terrific person ever', are good examples. So, the next stage to becoming UB is learning how to talk and what to say.

How To Talk

1. Learn how to talk in English, otherwise you won't be able to understand the rest of this book. All the other languages sound funny anyway.

2. Start to talk with your mouth open, close it when you're finished and move it up and down in the middle.

3. Remember to breathe while you're talking, otherwise you'll die.

4. Talk to yourself whenever you get the chance. It's a good way of finding out what you've been doing all day.

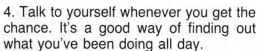

5. Make sure people listen to what you are saying by always talking through a loud speaker.

6. Never eat your words, they'll make you burp.

7. Don't talk out of the back of your head – you'll get hairs in your mouth.

Out of all the words in the English language my favourite word is '*bleugh*' because it just so happens I invented it. And it wasn't difficult either. I just took the first letter of each word that described me best:

B → BRILLIANT
L → LEARNED
E → EARTHSHAKING
U → UTTERLY
G → GREAT
H → HEXTRAORDINARY

It's a terrific word and you can use it any time of day. Just take a deep breath — puff your mouth a bit and let it all slide out. B L E U G H.... It just rolls off the face like slime.

BLEUGH

✱✱✱✱✱✱✱✱✱✱✱✱✱✱✱✱✱✱✱✱✱✱✱✱✱✱

61

FACTS ABOUT LANGUAGE

If you wanted to you could talk to approximately 400 million people in the world who would understand what you were on about. (*Unless you were explaining the rules of Mallett's Mallet.*)

There is a tribe of Mexican Indians who talk to each other by whistling. English is spoken in at least 45 countries. This is more than any other language. About one third of the world speaks it. (*The other two thirds are thick.*)

There are about one million words in the English language. More than in any other language.
By the time you get to be as utterly brilliant as me you will have used roughly 10,000 different words. (*Tick 'em off as you use 'em*).

There is a scientific word in the English language which is 207,000 letters long. (*But I can't remember what it is!*)

Now if you're not doing anything utterly brilliant this afternoon, how about inventing your own word. It's not difficult. In fact it was my great grandfather, an Indian chief named Old Keokuk Mallett, who invented the word OK, simply by taking the initials of his own name. Most people these days prefer to say TM, however.

Timmy Mallett's TOP 10 Favourite Words

BLEUGH

UTTERLY

BRILLIANT

BOTTY

BONKERS

SPLODGE

ME

GRONG DOOLY WANG

SPLAT

SPLERGE

Now if you're thinking of going abroad this summer it's a good idea to be able to say **bleugh** in different languages. It's an internationally known word and is a lot less boring than saying 'Hi'. Here's how to say **bleugh** to your foreign friends.

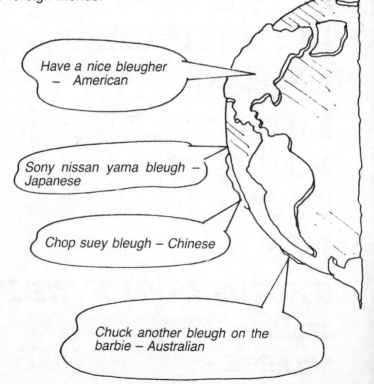

Have a nice bleugher
    – American

Sony nissan yama bleugh – Japanese

Chop suey bleugh – Chinese

Chuck another bleugh on the barbie – Australian

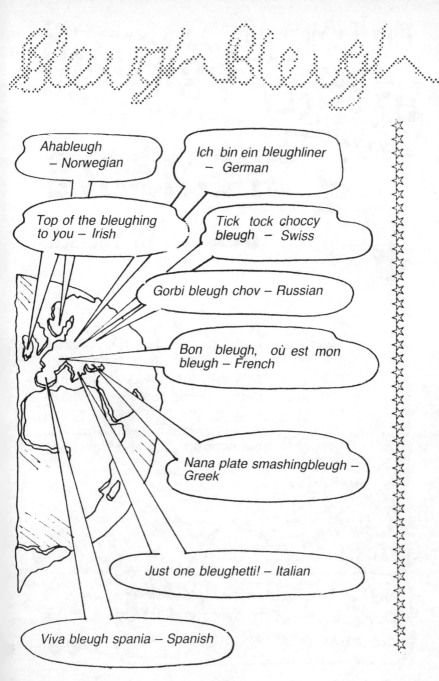

65

How To Make An

UTTERLY BRILLIANT

SPECTACLE

Of Yourself

The easiest way to make an utterly brilliant spectacle of yourself is to wear specs, like me! I got my first pair when I was seven and from then onwards there was no looking back. It was just great to be able to go 'hurr' all over the lenses to clean them. Now I've got over 50 pairs and I love 'em all.

And, just to make non-spectacled people even more annoyed, here are some more annoying facts:-

Wearing glasses means you've got something to talk to the Queen about.

Wearing glasses means you can see, (this is useful if you want to look at something).

Wearing glasses means your nose has something to look up to.

Wearing glasses means you can get all steamed up in the bath.

Wearing glasses stops you getting poked in the eye with a sharp stick.

Wearing glasses means you'll always look brainy.

WELL-KNOWN FACT

It's a well known fact that the only reason we have a nose and two ears is so we can hang a pair of glasses on them. People who don't wear glasses soon find that their nose becomes lazy and fat, and their ears start hanging about all over the place.

WEARING GLASSES

MEANS YOU CAN BECOME

- *Glass*-wegian
- A *Spec*-ialist
- A *Spec*-imen
- A *Glass*-blower
- A *Spec*-tator
- *Spec*-tacular
- A *Glass*-house
- A *Spec*-ial case
- A *Spec*-k
- A *Spec*-ies

WHAT DID ONE EYE SAY TO THE OTHER EYE?

BETWEEN YOU AND ME – SOMETHING SMELLS!

HOW TO MAKE YOUR OWN GLASSES

1. Remove two large windows from your house.

2. Join them in the middle with something soft - like your bed.

3. Attach one firm floor board or small tree to each side of glass (making sure these rest comfortably on your ears).

4. 'Hurr' on both panes of glass to clean before wearing.

⭐Utterly Brilliant Inventors⭐
and How To Become One

An easy way to become utterly brilliant is to invent something that no one else in the entire universe has ever thought of. Anyone can do it, as long as they have an utterly inventive mind, like me.

I normally like to invent at least one brilliant thing a day. In fact only yesterday I invented a new way of standing on my head (see drawing).

HELPFUL HINT

Don't set your sights too high. Nearly all the famous inventors started off inventing small things, like Alexander Graham Bell for instance who, on his first day as an inventor, came up with the telephone. A bit daft really but it came in quite handy when he wanted to tell his friends about it.

It also helps if invention runs in your family. And it just happens to run in mine. Here are some of the brilliant things invented by my ancestors.

Crisps

One day in 1867, in Saratoga, USA, Chuck Butch Wayne Mallett accidentally dropped a couple of thinly sliced potatoes into some hot cooking oil, and before he could say 'I hope no one ever invents crisps,' the whole world was eating them. The first crisp factory was opened in New York in 1925.

Spectacles

Glasses were originally called 'discs for eyes', and invented by an unknown glassworker (probably called Mallettini) from Italy between 1280 and 1286. At first they were only made for the long-sighted, and short-sighted people like me didn't get a look in until two hundred years later. What a SPECtacular invention!

The Fork

Perriwinkle Mallett returned from a holiday in Italy in 1608 and showed his friends an Italian eating stick called the fork. At first everyone thought it was a joke, and preferred to carry on eating with their fingers (peasants) until King James I of Mallett used it in 1588, and then everyone wanted one. Good FORK him!

Now as you'll agree, all these inventions are fairly simple and extremely boring, I mean who wants to be famous for inventing a fork? So I suggest that whatever you invent must be utterly original and brilliantly useful. Here are ten things that I invented last week:—

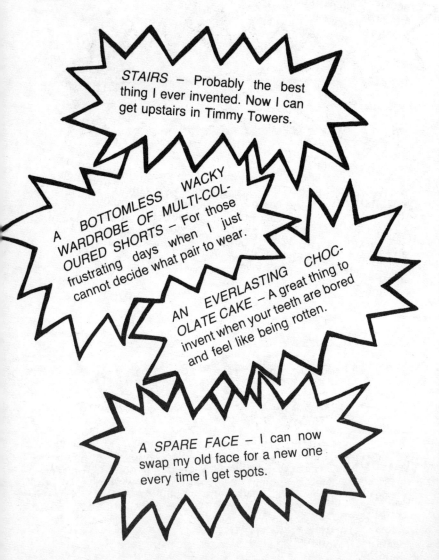

STAIRS – Probably the best thing I ever invented. Now I can get upstairs in Timmy Towers.

A BOTTOMLESS WACKY WARDROBE OF MULTI-COLOURED SHORTS – For those frustrating days when I just cannot decide what pair to wear.

AN EVERLASTING CHOCOLATE CAKE – A great thing to invent when your teeth are bored and feel like being rotten.

A *SPARE FACE* – I can now swap my old face for a new one every time I get spots.

AN ENCYCLOPEDIA OF GREAT EXCUSES – So you never have to do the washing up ever again.

AIR – Very handy for breathing and blowing up rubber rings.

AN AUTOMATIC FAN CLUB – Of course I invented this for a friend. At the touch of a button he can summon a crowd of 10,000 to appear from round the corner.

TAPS – So I can put them on my feet and tap dance.

DOORS – Brilliant for opening and closing.

A DO-IT-YOURSELF HOME-WORK BOOK – Saving the world from homework has given me international fame and fortune. I simply tell the teacher to 'do it yourself!' And I don't have any more homework.

The Utterly Brilliant Mallett's Mallet

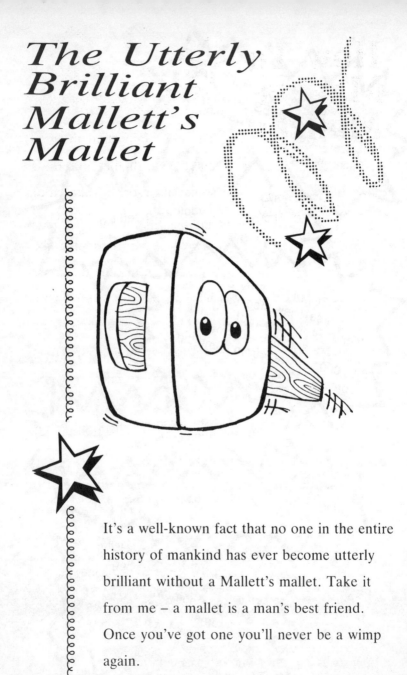

It's a well-known fact that no one in the entire
history of mankind has ever become utterly
brilliant without a Mallett's mallet. Take it
from me – a mallet is a man's best friend.
Once you've got one you'll never be a wimp
again.

How To Make a Mallet

The most important thing to make your mallet out of is something soft – like your mum, cotton wool, paper, stewed apple or soup. The softer your mallet, the more comfortable you will feel with it, and the lighter it will be to carry around. Dress it in bright colours like black and decker, so it can be seen at night or camouflaged quickly in a bowl of rhubarb and gravy during the day.

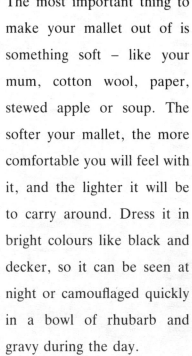

☆ With Your Mallet

I've done exactly 6 squillion 837,324 different things with my mallet and here's 10 more you can do with yours:–

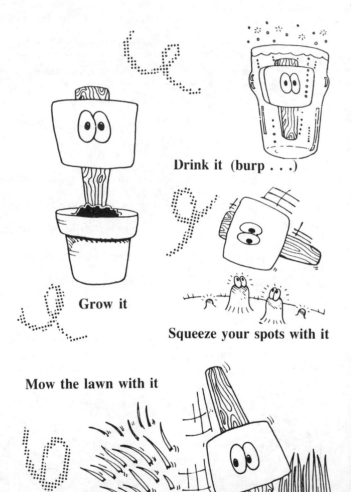

Drink it (burp . . .)

Grow it

Squeeze your spots with it

Mow the lawn with it

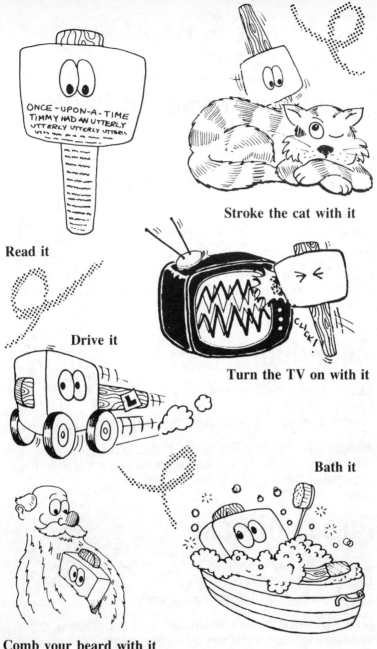

ONCE-UPON-A-TIME
TIMMY HAD AN UTTERLY
UTTERLY UTTERLY UTTERLY

Read it

Stroke the cat with it

Drive it

Turn the TV on with it

CLICK!

Bath it

Comb your beard with it

YOUR STARS... ☆☆
with extraterrestrial Timmy

Capricorn on the cob

Lucky stone – cobble
Lucky teeth – missing front ones
Lucky number – 3,548,729

Looks like you've bitten off more than you can chew this month. Good advice is to I-GNAW the past, turn a CORN-ER and bite into a whole new area.

Aquarium

Lucky food – fish fingers
Lucky pet – fish
Lucky number – you haven't got one

People who live in glass houses should live somewhere else is my motto. All the Aquariums I know are wet. Go and make friends with some tadpoles.

Pisces of Cake

Lucky bath toy – sponge
Lucky shop – bakers
Lucky period in history – icing age

An utterly brilliant sign. You're the sort of person who can have his cake and eat everyone else's . The next step is to make your friends look up to you. Try wearing a pair of stilts.

Aries rock

Lucky country – Australia
Lucky hobby – rock climbing
Lucky food – rock

Don't move. Don't look behind you. Stand completely still for several million years! (Or try making friends with a bread roll, then you can rock and roll!)

Taurus the bully

Lucky colour – red
Unlucky country – Spain
Unlucky game – darts

When you grow up you will work in a china shop. Until then – be very wary of fields that are round and anyone wearing a red coat.

Gemini was Born Under a Wandering Star

Lucky stone – Mick Jagger
Lucky biscuit – Macaroon
Lucky shoe – open-toe sandal

Stay in bed all month. In your condition it just ain't worth getting up. But don't look under the bed – the alligator is still there and he's very hungry.

Crabby

Lucky sandwich filling – crab paste
Lucky furniture – shelf
Unlucky hobby -- fishing

IF TODAY IS YOUR BIRTHDAY: So what! You're not the only one mate, so scarper. And don't expect a present from me. You SHELLFISH person

Leo-E-I-O

Lucky meal – head
Lucky holiday resort – jungle
Lucky film – 'Claws 2'

Be sure to follow your hunches or they will start following you. And then you will look a bit daft won't you?

Virgo and Get a New Hair Style

Unlucky glass – mirror
Unlucky hairstyle – yours
Lucky item of clothing – big hat

Despite the way you look, you are regarded as flavour of the month by your friends. Either they have terrible taste or they think you are a sucker.

Libra bah black sheep

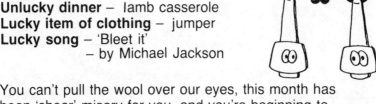

Unlucky dinner – lamb casserole
Lucky item of clothing – jumper
Lucky song – 'Bleet it'
                – by Michael Jackson

You can't pull the wool over our eyes, this month has been 'shear' misery for you, and you're beginning to look a bit sheepish. I suggest a new flock of friends – or even a pen pal! Why not write to your biro?

Scorpion

Lucky stone – a big one
Lucky pop singer – Sting
Lucky swimming stroke – crawl

If you really want your bite to be worse than your bark you need to get out of the habit of creeping up on people and pinching things. It's time to come out of your shell and reveal what you're really made of.

Sagitearaway

Lucky food – sprout and chocolate yoghurt
Lucky for you – people don't know you're as daft as you look.
Unlucky for you – I do! However, I do have a soft spot for you, it's a swamp at the bottom of my garden!

Are You Still Utterly Stupid?

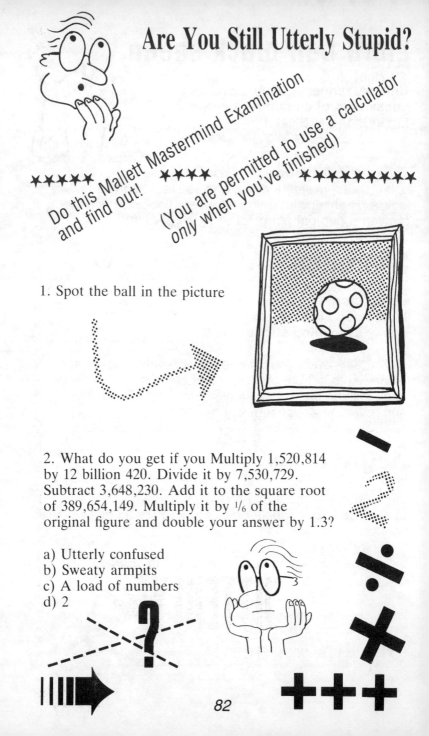

★★★★★ ★★★★ (You are permitted to use a calculator only when you've finished) ★★★★★★★★★★

1. Spot the ball in the picture

2. What do you get if you Multiply 1,520,814 by 12 billion 420. Divide it by 7,530,729. Subtract 3,648,230. Add it to the square root of 389,654,149. Multiply it by ⅙ of the original figure and double your answer by 1.3?

a) Utterly confused
b) Sweaty armpits
c) A load of numbers
d) 2

82

3. What is the correct use of grammar?

a) The yolk of an egg *ARE* white
b) The yolk of an egg *WERE* white
c) The yolk of an egg *MIGHT BE* white
d) *IS* the yolk of an egg white? (of course it isn't, you nit)

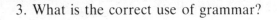

4. Which of the following shapes has three sides?

a)

c)

b)

d)

5. If your answer is what is the question?

a) Are you thick?
b) Can you spell corectly?
c) Have you had enough of this quiz?
d) Are you using a calculator (cheat)?

6. Make 10 other words out of the word

(Your answers should not include the words: UT, ER, UTTER, LY, TE or ERLT.)

7. Make 20 other words out of the word

BRILLIANT

(Your answer should not include the words: BRILL, ANT, LIAN, BRI, ILLI, NT, RILL or ILLIANT.)

8. Which of these two lines is the longest?

a) ▬▬▬▬▬▬▬   b) ▬▬▬▬▬▬▬

9. You are about to hear two noises. Which was the loudest?

a) The first one
b) The one that followed

10. The two words below have been written in invisible ink. What are they?

a)

b)

Answers on a Postage Stamp

UTTERLY BRILLIANT

OCCUPATIONS

HOW TO BECOME

PRIME MINISTER

a) Vote for yourself – a lot.

b) Sit in a cabinet.

c) Give all your friends a job and then sack them.

d) Learn how to wave.

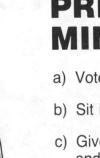

HOW TO BE  A SPACEMAN

a) Find a space.

b) Cover yourself in tinfoil.

c) Speak with a crackly voice, bleep a lot and keep saying "Houston".

d) Learn to float on the ceiling.

HOW TO BE
● ● ● A PIRATE

a) Find an eye patch. If this is difficult a cabbage patch or patchwork quilt will do.

b) Buy or borrow a shoulder that you can stuff and pin to your parrot.

WHAT DO SHARKS SAY WHEN THEY'RE HUNGRY?

I'M STARFIN!

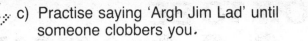

c) Practise saying 'Argh Jim Lad' until someone clobbers you.

d) Fold your left leg at the knee, hide it in a safe place and replace it with a wooden stick.

e) Find a deserted island where you can frighten people.

BURP!

PESKY VEGETARIAN SHARKS.....
..THEY'VE EATEN MY SHIP!

HOW TO BE

● ● ● A POP STAR

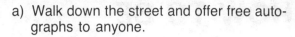

a) Walk down the street and offer free autographs to anyone.

b) Practise dancing on a hedgehog.

c) Write to Top of the Pops and say you won't watch it again until you are on.

d) Look out of the window and call yourself after the first thing you see. "Hedge, Hedge, Hedge" is a good example.

e) Give your clothes to the dog to chew up. Wear the dog for your first concert.

HOW TO BE A VAMPIRE

a) Grow your teeth an inch longer.

b) Refuse to get out of bed in the morning if the sun's shining. If it's not – pretend.

c) Paint tomato ketchup on everything.

d) Ask if you can do Transylvanian 'O' level at school. If they refuse – bite them.

In case you have failed to notice, this is the first ever multi-purpose book, and once it's served its term as a thing to read, there is an unlimited supply of things you can do with it. For instance:–

● Sell it to someone else as a birthday present.

HAPPY BIRTHDAY

THANK YOU

● Buy 2 and throw one away.

● Feed it to your next-door neighbour.

● Attach it to a piece of string and fly it as a kite.

TIMMY MALLETT'S UTTERLY BRILLIANT BOOK

TIMMY MALLETT'S UTTERLY FROZEN BOOK

● Put it in the freezer so you can read it again next year.

● Wear it.

● Put legs on it and convert it into a small table.

● Knit it into a cardi for your granny.

● Attach a stick to it and use it as a book attached to a stick.

● Show it to your hamster.

TIMMY MALLETT'S UTTERLY BRILLIANT BOOK

TIMMY MALLETTS UTTERLY BRILLIANT HAMSTER BOOK

● Put it down your trousers and take it out again.

● Bury it and see if it turns into a tree.

● Read it all over again. (If you haven't got anything more useful to do than this – you need to!)